"*The Adventure of Christmas* is a remarkable achievement. With captivating illustrations and a simple but compelling approach to storytelling, Ed Drew has written an inspiring Advent devotional, grace-filled and truth-soaked and entirely approachable. Each page from the Christmas story comes to life, and the questions and activities are thoughtful but not over-burdensome. I'm so grateful for this new doorway into Advent season with my family."

RANDALL GOODGAME, Slugs and Bugs; Author,
Jesus and the Very Big Surprise

"When you take a journey with children, you pack for every possibility. This devotional does just that as it walks families through the unchangeable map of Advent with questions and activities to engage even the most restless traveler."

CHERYCE BERG, Director of Children's Ministries,
College Church, Wheaton

"Another great resource for families from Faith in Kids! With its age-specific questions, there's something here to help you celebrate Jesus whatever stage your family is at. Ed writes with an unwavering commitment to God's word, a healthy dose of fun and realistic expectations about family life. This is a brilliant way to plan your 'Adventure' this Christmas."

DAN ADAMS AND GARETH LOH, Awesome Cutlery

"A short but meaningful daily Advent family devotional with something for all ages from under-5s to adults!"

VICTORIA BEECH, GodVenture

"A wonderful book which equips the whole family to discover the Christmas story afresh."

KATHARINE HILL, Director, Care for the Family

"It's so easy for us all to get distracted with busyness over the Christmas period. As a family, these simple but profound sessions took us deeper into the Christmas story, gave us a rhythm for reflection and sparked more faith conversations with our kids."

ANDY AND JO FROST, Share Jesus International
and the Evangelical Alliance

"'Wow!' That's what I thought when I stepped into *The Adventure Of Christmas*! Wow—it's such a well-thought-through and cleverly-designed guide for families of all ages! Wow—it's so easy to use! Wow—what wise and helpful and practical words! And this amazing adventure leads so beautifully and wonderfully to the biggest wow of all—the baby in the manger, our Saviour and King, Jesus!"

COLIN BUCHANAN, Musician

"What do our kids need this Christmas? More than anything they need to know and love God. Ed Drew helps make discipling our family easier—no matter what the age range! *The Adventure of Christmas* is truly the gift that keeps on giving."

BARBARA REAOCH, Author, *A Jesus Christmas*

"Faith in Kids have such a huge heart for encouraging the whole family to explore faith and they come up with so many great ways to do just that. *The Adventure of Christmas* is no exception. Simple enough to make it easy for any family to use but also packed with creative ideas, question starters for any age and lots of optional extras, this is a really helpful way to make the most of Advent together as a family."

LOU WOOLCOCK, Families Co-ordinator, Youth for Christ

Ed Drew

THE ADVENTURE OF CHRISTMAS

*A journey through Advent
for the whole family*

thegoodbook
COMPANY

The Adventure of Christmas
© Faith in Kids 2021. Reprinted 2022 (twice).
www.faithinkids.org

Published by:
The Good Book Company

thegoodbook.com | thegoodbook.co.uk
thegoodbook.com.au | thegoodbook.co.nz | thegoodbook.co.in

Unless otherwise indicated, Scriptures quoted from the International Children's Bible®, copyright ©1986, 1988, 1999, 2015 by Tommy Nelson. Used by permission.

Cover and design by André Parker | Illustrations and icons by Alex Webb-Peploe

ISBN: 9781784986520 | Printed in India

 # Contents

Before you begin

The first Christmas was an adventure like no other.

The angels blazed brighter than any Christmas lights. Elizabeth and Zechariah's joy at their baby was beyond any grandparents' delight at a kids' Christmas play. Mary's preparation was more chaotic than any festive family gathering. Joseph's journey to Bethlehem was harder than any road trip to relatives. The shepherd's midnight arrival, bursting into the silence, was more entertaining than any family film night. The wise men's gifts were more precious than any sparkly wrapped present. King Herod's anger was more extreme than any family row you have witnessed.

Let the incredible adventure of the first Christmas light up your Advent.

In this book you will find 25 sessions. They're designed to start on 1st December and finish on Christmas Day—but they don't have to be used that way. Not all families will manage a Bible time every day; if you get behind, skip over the ones you missed and pick up the story or just catch up after Christmas.

We have written each Bible time to take you less than ten minutes. So find a place and a time to give yourselves ten minutes each day to listen, think, talk and pray. The sessions start with a prayer and a question to get your family going in the right direction. Then there are a few sentences to introduce where we are in the Bible and one idea to listen out for. You will be reading a few verses from Luke's and Matthew's Gospels. For families with young children there is usually an extra suggestion for when you read the passage to try to engage them more in the story, because not many four-year-olds find it easy to sit still for ten minutes. (But one day they will…) There's a question for each age group and a prayer suggestion to finish. After that there are a few optional sections to enjoy on the journey to school or in a moment before bedtime. Make it work for your family, because the Lord has made every family different.

God bless your family as you enjoy the adventure of Christmas together.

Top tips

- Doing a study a day until Christmas can be a challenge when December is so busy. You could just do the key stories to make it more manageable—these are marked with a star in the top right-hand corner. If you fall behind, you have not failed. Do the right studies on Christmas Eve and Christmas Day, and keep going with the others—if necessary, into January!

- Each day there are four questions, differentiated by age. Usually each day's questions build on each other, to develop the big idea. So while the questions are aimed at the different age ranges, it will work best if you run through the earlier questions even if you don't have children of that age. And you know your kids better than I do, so if you think they will be able to think about the questions in categories older than their age, go ahead and keep going through the questions! Adults can answer questions too—see next point!

- Remember that there is huge value in your children seeing their parents answering questions from the Bible, talking about their faith, showing that they don't have all the answers, and praying. It will have a lasting impact for children to see their parents engaging with the Bible, humbly accepting that they are a work in progress and praying to their own heavenly Father.

- Each day's reading has a suggestion for younger children to help them to engage with it. Under-5's need extra help to grasp what is happening in the story. There is a picture for each day. Ask your child to identify the people in the picture and to describe the action. You could use toy action figures to make a drama out of each story. This age group would be helped by having a children's picture Bible to see what is happening in the Bible stories. The Beginner's Bible and the Jesus Storybook Bible are good for this.

- There's a separate "Adventure of Christmas Calendar", with stickers, that goes alongside this book. You don't need it to enjoy these devotionals! But if you'd like one, you'll find it at thegoodbook.co.uk/adventurecal or thegoodbook. com/adventurecal.

If your family are new to family Bible times, or if you are restarting them after a break and you face some opposition to the idea, here are a few things you might find helpful:

- You could set a timer for ten minutes (and hide it, so that the ticking seconds aren't watched!) and promise that when the alarm goes off, you will stop the conversation and everyone will pray in response. Keep that promise, no matter how far you've got. (If your children are currently more malleable, then don't use a timer, as it may set an expectation that the ten minutes will be a form of a torture.)

- Set an expectation that this time together will be the highlight of the day. Jesus likened God's words in the Bible to bread (Matthew 4:4)—your family needs this ten minutes each day to survive just as much as they need food to eat. When you have finished a Bible time, find reasons to praise your child or to highlight a success. Let them know that their engagement, understanding and enthusiasm matter to you.

- Ask your children to help make the decisions about how your family Bible times will work (not whether they will happen—that's your call, not theirs—but how they will happen).

  - What time do we want them?

  - Where do we want them to happen so that they are a great opportunity to learn and concentrate?

  - What will need to be done before we can sit down together each day?

  - What role can each of us play to make them happen?

- Don't be disappointed if not every day feels easy or enthusiastic. If you can manage to do three or four family Bible times so that there is a sense of an expectation and a routine, then they will usually improve. As always with children, there will be days that are a struggle. Those days will show you your need of Jesus Christ in your parenting—which is no bad thing!

- Change the plan if the plan isn't working.

God bless you in this. Take a moment to pray for your efforts. If you don't already feel dependent on Jesus Christ in your parenting, you are about to!

DAY	PASSAGE	TITLE	KEY WORD
1	Luke 1 v 1-4	The eyes that saw	**Luke**
2	Luke 1 v 5-10	Zechariah & Elizabeth	**Zechariah & Elizabeth**
3	Luke 1 v 11-17	One to go before the Lord	**Get ready**
4	Luke 1 v 18-25	No words to explain	**Believe!**
5	Luke 1 v 26-27	A girl named Mary	**Mary**
6	Luke 1 v 28-33	A baby with a throne	**King**
7	Luke 1 v 34-38	How?	**Son of God**
8	Matt 1 v 18-19	A boy named Joseph	**Joseph**
9	Matt 1 v 20-21	He will save us	**Save**
10	Matt 1 v 22-25	God with us	**Immanuel**
11	Luke 1 v 39-45	Leaping for joy	**Blessed**
12	Luke 2 v 1-5	Off to Bethlehem	**Bethlehem**
13	Luke 2 v 6-7	The big birth	**Born!**
14	Luke 2 v 8-12	Burning up the night	**Shepherds**
15	Luke 2 v 13-14	Turn up the music	**Praise**
16	Luke 2 v 15-17a	See the baby	**Seen**
17	Luke 2 v 17b-20	Sharing the story	**Tell**
18	Luke 2 v 25-33	A promise kept	**Simeon**
19	Luke 2 v 36-38	A very focused widow	**Anna**
20	Matt 2 v 1-3	Men from the east	**Wise men**
21	Matt 2 v 4-8	To Bethlehem	**Herod**
22	Matt 2 v 9-12	On your knees	**Worship**
23	Luke 2 v 39-40	A strong and gracious Saviour	**Growing**
24	Luke 2 v 16-18	Back to the manger	**Amazed**
25	Recap	Merry Christmas!	**The King has come**

Note: The **KEY STORIES** are the ones marked with a star.

How to use the Advent calendar

On the opposite page you'll see a "calendar" with a key word or phrase and an icon for each day. These words will help you to remember where you've been.

Your child might also like to colour in each day as you finish it. Maybe they could choose some Christmas colours or glitter pens.

You can also download and print out a version of this calendar from www.thegoodbook.com/the-adventure-of-christmas. You could suspend a piece of string or ribbon across the room where you'll do your Bible times, cut out the calendar icons, and then hang them up on the string/ribbon day by day.

Advent Calendar

DAY 1

The eyes that saw

⊙ Where are we going today?
We can trust what we read, because Luke spoke to those who met Jesus and then wrote down exactly what happened.

Pray: Dear Father, thank you that we can get ready for Christmas by hearing what really happened during that first Christmas. Amen.

Ask a quick question
What is the most amazing thing you have ever seen with your own eyes?

Link: Today we're going to see that Luke spoke to those who saw what happened that first Christmas. He wrote down exactly what they told him.

Today's story
- *Where are we in the Bible?* This is the very start of Luke's true story of Jesus' life. Luke starts by explaining how he wrote his Gospel and why. He's writing to an important friend (who he calls "your Excellency") who was a follower of Jesus.

- *Look out for* why Luke says we can trust what we read in his Gospel.

- *Read the passage. For young children, use the pictures to explain as you read.*

Luke 1 v 1-4
¹ Many have tried to give a history of the things that happened among us. ² They have written the same things that we learned from others—the people who saw those things from the beginning and served God by telling people his message. ³ I myself studied everything carefully from

the beginning, your Excellency. I thought I should write it out for you. So I put it in order in a book. ⁴ I write these things so that you can know that what you have been taught is true.

--- ❓ ---

Question for 3s and 4s
Look at today's pictures. Luke is talking to people who met Jesus. Can you see where Luke is writing their story on his tablet?

Question for 5-7s
Listen to verse 4: "I write these things so that you can know that what you have been taught is true". Why did Luke want to write his Gospel? (*Luke wrote his Gospel so that his readers could be certain that what they had heard about Jesus was true. He spoke to the people who had seen Jesus in the flesh, teaching and doing miracles. Luke made sure that every detail in his Gospel about Jesus really happened.*)

Question for over-7s
Look at verse 2. From which people did Luke find out about what happened? What do you think Luke actually had to do to write his Gospel? (*Finding out what really happened is not as easy as it sounds. How did Luke find those eyewitnesses? People remember different details. There were no videos or photos, just the memories of people who were there to see Jesus. But Luke "studied everything carefully" and pieced it all together.*)

Question for teens
Is Luke's method different to how most people assume that the Bible came to be written, do you think? How does Luke's method change how we view his story of the first Christmas? (*We're not reading myth or legend. We're not reading what a bunch of early Christians made up one dark night. We are reading the facts of the first Christmas. We're reading history!*)

Think and pray
Pray asking God to help you as you learn from Luke's Gospel. Thank God for how Luke wrote his Gospel.

Want to get baking?

Make some edible eyewitness eyeballs! They could be made from marshmallows with chocolate buttons stuck on the top using chocolate spread, or a biscuit with a splodge of coloured icing and a chocolate chip in the middle.

Got time to chat?

Have you ever wondered how much of the story of the first Christmas is really history? With school Christmas productions, endless Christmas films and hundreds of years of traditions, it can be hard to work out what is made up and what is history. Do you think it matters?

Something more for the adults?

Sooner or later, we will be asked questions about the trustworthiness of the Bible. Some of those we know will just dismiss the Bible and our belief in it. We believe that at the first Christmas God became a baby who grew up to walk, talk, eat, cry and listen. Through the certainty of knowing about Jesus, we can decide to trust him as our Lord. Thank God for the certainty we can have in who Jesus really is.

DAY 2

Zechariah and Elizabeth

⊙ Where are we going today?
Elizabeth and Zechariah lived good lives for God. They had no children.

Pray: Dear Father, thank you that in the Bible we meet the people who were part of your plan for that first Christmas. Amen.

❓ Ask a quick question
Do you know an elderly couple? What are they like?

Link: Today we're going to see an amazing elderly couple. Enjoy meeting them.

Today's story
- *Where are we in the Bible?* It's been 400 years since God last spoke to his people. No prophets. No angels. No words. But some of God's people are still trusting God in spite of the silence.

- *Look out for the joy and the sadness of this elderly couple.*

- *Read the passage. For young children, point out the characters in the picture as you read. You could stop after verse 7.*

Luke 1 v 5-10
⁵ *During the time Herod ruled Judea, there was a priest named Zechariah. He belonged to Abijah's group. Zechariah's wife came from the family of Aaron. Her name was Elizabeth.* ⁶ *Zechariah and Elizabeth truly did what God said was good. They did everything the Lord commanded and told*

people to do. They were without fault in keeping his law. ⁷ But Zechariah and Elizabeth had no children. Elizabeth could not have a baby; and both of them were very old.

⁸ Zechariah was serving as a priest before God for his group. It was his group's time to serve. ⁹ According to the custom of the priests, he was chosen to go into the Temple of the Lord and burn incense. ¹⁰ There were a great many people outside praying at the time the incense was offered.

--- **?** ---

Question for 3s and 4s
Why might Elizabeth and Zechariah have sometimes felt sad?

Question for 5-7s
Look at verses 8-10. What exciting thing was Zechariah going to do that day? *(What an honour! Tomorrow we'll find out what happened when Zechariah went into the Temple.)*

Question for over-7s
Read verse 6. If that's what Elizabeth and Zechariah were like, what kinds of things do you think they did each day?

Question for teens
If you could meet Zechariah and Elizabeth at this point in their lives, what question would you ask them? What question might they have asked God?

 Think and pray
Zechariah and Elizabeth kept living for God, doing good. Pray that God would help you to do the same.

! OPTIONAL EXTRAS

Want to get busy?

Can you think of an elderly couple in your church who live for God as Zechariah and Elizabeth did? They would love to hear that their goodness reminds you of Zechariah and Elizabeth. Give them a ring or send them a card. They'll be so pleased to hear from you.

Got time to chat?

It makes our hearts ache to hear that Zechariah and Elizabeth were so good and yet still life hurt so much. We sometimes think that if we serve God, he will make life easy for us. As Luke's Gospel continues, we are going to see how God uses Zechariah and Elizabeth's hurt for his glorious plan. Could God use your hurt for his glorious plan?

Something more for the adults?

Elizabeth says in 1 v 25, "In these days he has shown his favour and taken away my disgrace among the people" (NIV). Notice that word "dis-grace"? Sometimes God's grace appears to be missing in our painful circumstances. But at the first Christmas, God showed his favour to a hurting world. Pray that this Christmas God's favour might shine into the hurt and dis-grace of your life, and of those around you.

DAY 3

One to go before the Lord

 Where are we going today?
The angel promised Zechariah and Elizabeth a special son who would grow up to get the people ready for Jesus.

Pray: Dear Father, please get us ready for celebrating Jesus' birth. Amen.

Ask a quick question
Can you think of five ways that our family gets ready for Christmas? How do we prepare for Christmas?

Link: In today's story we're going to find out how God got the people ready for the first Christmas.

Today's story
- *Where are we in the Bible?* Zechariah and Elizabeth were old, godly and hurting from having no children. That day, Zechariah was stepping into the heart of God's Temple, for the only time in his life.

- *Look out for* the job God had for their amazing baby.

- *Read the passage. For young children, just read the* **bold text.**

Luke 1 v 11-17
¹¹ Then, on the right side of the incense table, an angel of the Lord came and stood before Zechariah. ¹² When he saw the angel, Zechariah was confused and frightened. ¹³ But the angel said to him,

21

"Zechariah, don't be afraid. Your prayer has been heard by God. Your wife, Elizabeth, will give birth to a son. You will name him John. [14] *You will be very happy. Many people will be happy because of his birth.* [15] *John will be a great man for the Lord. He will never drink wine or beer. Even at the time John is born, he will be filled with the Holy Spirit.* [16] **He will help many people of Israel return to the Lord their God.** [17] *He himself will go first before the Lord. John will be powerful in spirit like Elijah. He will make peace between fathers and their children. He will bring those who are not obeying God back to the right way of thinking.* **He will make people ready for the coming of the Lord."**

―――――――――――――― ❓ ――――――――――――――

Question for 3s and 4s
How did Zechariah feel when the angel appeared?

Question for 5-7s
What a day Zechariah had! What do you think was his biggest surprise?

Question for over-7s
Listen again to what the angel said John would do. *(Read verses 16-17.)* What would John get people ready for?

Question for teens
In verse 17 it says that part of John's job would be making peace between fathers and their children. When we return to the Lord, how does that change our relationship with God—and how might that change our relationship with our family? *(If we aren't at peace with God, we can't find peace with people either. But when people return to the Lord, they have peace with him—then the Lord gives them a peace with others. Families who have all come home to the Lord will love one another more.)*

――――――――――――――――――――――――

Think and pray
Pray that as your family gets ready for Christmas with fairy lights and presents under a tree, you'd also be ready for the coming of our Lord.

! OPTIONAL EXTRAS

Want to get crafty?

Make a decoration for your tree to say that you're ready for Jesus to come again. Decorate a crown shape and write across it, "We're ready!"

Got time to chat?

After reading this story, and thinking about what John's job is going to be, it makes us wonder how ready we are for Jesus. If you had to get your road, village or town ready for the arrival of a king or queen, what sort of things would you do? A bit of painting? Put up some flags? But if John had to get your road, village or town ready for the arrival of the Lord, what sort of things do you think he would do?

Something more for the adults?

Today we heard the first words God had said to his people for 400 years. Let's hear the very last words God spoke 400 years earlier: the last words of the Old Testament. Hear the echoes with the angel's message. Hear the tone that suggests the coming of the Lord will not be good news for everyone. Pray that this Christmas some would be made ready for the coming of the Lord for the first time.

> [5] See, I will send the prophet Elijah to you before that great and dreadful day of the LORD comes. [6] He will turn the hearts of the parents to their children, and the hearts of the children to their parents; or else I will come and strike the land with total destruction. (Malachi 4 v 5-6, NIV)

DAY 4

No words to explain

 ## Where are we going today?

God's word can be believed when it looks impossible. The angel taught Zechariah this by stopping him from speaking until John was born.

Pray: Dear Father, please help us to know that your words are true even when they seem hard to believe. Amen.

Ask a quick question

Do you know a true story or fact that seems too incredible to be true?

Link: Today Zechariah finds it hard to believe what God was saying.

Today's story

- *Where are we in the Bible?* Zechariah and Elizabeth had no children and were now too old to have any. But the angel had told Zechariah that God was about to change that. Elizabeth would soon have a child called John.

- *Look out for what Zechariah thinks of this news.*

- *Read the passage. For young children, grab some toy figures (or spice jars!) to tell the story as you read the passage.*

Luke 1 v 18-25

[18] *Zechariah said to the angel, "How can I know that what you say is true? I am an old man, and my wife is old, too." [19] The angel answered him, "I am Gabriel. I stand before God. God sent me to talk to you and to tell you this good news. [20] Now, listen! You will not be able to talk until the day these things happen. You will lose your speech because you did not believe what I told you. But these things will really happen."*

[21] *Outside, the people were still waiting for Zechariah. They were*

surprised that he was staying so long in the Temple. [22] Then Zechariah came outside, but he could not speak to them. So they knew that he had seen a vision in the Temple. Zechariah could not speak. He could only make signs to them. [23] When his time of service as a priest was finished, he went home.

[24] Later, Zechariah's wife, Elizabeth, became pregnant. She did not go out of her house for five months. Elizabeth said, [25] "Look what the Lord has done for me! My people were ashamed of me, but now the Lord has taken away that shame."

Question for 3s and 4s

Zechariah didn't believe they would have a baby. What did the angel say would happen to Zechariah?

Question for 5-7s

Why didn't Zechariah believe that Elizabeth would have a baby?

Question for over-7s

What did God do to help Zechariah to believe God's word? (*God sent an angel. God took away Zechariah's words to make him listen more. And God did the miracle of making Elizabeth pregnant. How kind!*)

Question for teens

Listen to Zechariah's answer to the angel: "How can I know that what you say is true?" Have you ever thought that about something in the Bible? (Ask an adult when they last thought that!) Have another look at Gabriel's answer in verses 19-20. How might it help us when we find it hard to believe? (*There is so much to help us! First, the angel says it WILL happen, because God says it will. Simple! Second, if it has come from God, it is always GOOD NEWS. God's plan for our lives is always a better plan, so we can trust him. Third, God is so kind when we don't believe. He didn't destroy Zechariah or punish him; he gave him a sign to teach him, change him and help him. When we don't trust God, he doesn't punish us; he teaches us, changes us and helps us.*)

 Think and pray

Thank God for how kind he is when we find it hard to believe or pray that God would help you with a promise that you find hard to believe.

Want to get playing?

Have a quick round of charades. One person acts out a word or phrase without using any words. Zechariah had to live by doing charades—for months!

Got time to chat?

God's work in Zechariah's and Elizabeth's lives is miraculous, and it feels a long way from our own lives. But just like them, God is helping us to believe what once seemed impossible. Can we think of a promise we now believe that we didn't use to believe? Can we think of little (or big) examples of how the Spirit is changing and teaching us?

Something more for the adults?

Read Elizabeth's words in verse 25 again. Look at what we learn about our heavenly Father from these few words. He is the Lord who keeps his word and does what he says, even when it seems implausible, impossible or miraculous. He is the Lord who shows favour to the weakest. And most importantly, he is the Lord who takes away the disgrace of his people. Through Christ, he has removed our shame and wiped out our humiliation. Instead of the disgrace of judgment, the Lord gives us his loving care and compassion.

DAY 5

A girl named Mary

⊙ Where are we going today?
Meet Mary, a very ordinary teenager from a tiny little village. She was as ordinary as you and me.

Pray: Dear Father, please help us to see how Jesus came to ordinary people like us. Amen.

❓ Ask a quick question
What makes you ordinary? What makes you just like most people you know?

Link: Today we're going to see that God chose the most ordinary girl imaginable to be the mother of the most amazing baby ever.

Today's story
- *Where are we in the Bible?* We've just seen an angel announce to Zechariah that his wife, Elizabeth, will have a very special baby. Let's meet Elizabeth's relative, who was much younger than her.

- *Look out for* what we are told about Mary.

- *Read the passage. For young children, scatter some toy characters (or pasta) on the floor, explaining that this is the village of Nazareth. Pick one toy out, as God picked out Mary.*

Luke 1 v 26-27
26-27 *During Elizabeth's sixth month of pregnancy, God sent the angel Gabriel to a virgin who lived in Nazareth, a town in Galilee. She was engaged to marry a man named Joseph from the family of David. Her name was Mary.*

--- **?** ---

Question for 3s and 4s

Can you see the young woman in the picture? Did you hear what her name was? *(She's called Mary.)*

Question for 5-7s

What else are we told about Mary? Did you hear where she was from and who she was engaged to? *(She was from Nazareth, which was a tiny village. She was engaged to be married to Joseph.)*

Question for over-7s

The Son of God left his throne in heaven to be born from this woman. Can you imagine three ways that life in heaven's throne room would be different to life in the tiny village of Nazareth? *(Where to start?! In heaven Jesus was worshipped by angels, was equal with God the Father, had every privilege that he deserved, and had power and freedom to do whatever he chose. In the village of Nazareth he walked in dust, lived under a leaky roof, slept on an itchy bed, got bitten by insects. Giving up his freedom, he lived like Mary.)*

Question for teens

God could have chosen any important, rich or impressive woman to be the mother of Jesus. Why do you think he picked an ordinary teenager in a tiny village? *(Because Jesus didn't come for kings, princes, presidents and the rich—he came for the weak, the poor and the ordinary. He came for people like Mary, so he started his life living with Mary.)*

Think and pray

Thank God that Jesus understands what it is to be ordinary and poor, and how it feels to have parents.

! OPTIONAL EXTRAS

Want to get crafty?

Make a paperchain of young women, each one just like the others. Decorate one to be Mary. Colour in her face, stick on fabric for clothes, and find a way to give her hair.

Got time to chat?

Do you find yourselves looking at bigger houses, faster cars and brightly coloured shoes? Do you dream of being rich? Do you look differently at people with less money? Jesus could have had it all, but he chose to have nothing. He did not think less of people with less money. How did Jesus treat the poor? How did Jesus treat the rich?

Something more for the adults?

For you know the grace of our Lord Jesus Christ, that though he was rich, yet for your sake he became poor, so that you through his poverty might become rich. (2 Corinthians 8 v 9; NIV)

If Christ had chosen to be born into power and prestige, that would still have been an incredible sacrifice worth celebrating. But that he chose to be born into poverty is beyond our understanding. As we ponder his decision, we'll find ourselves treating others differently. We will take time with the needy. We will be patient with the weak. We will spend a little less time rubbing shoulders with the privileged.

Fun fact

Archaeologists are people who dig in the ground to find evidence of what a place used to be like. When they dug down in Nazareth, they found olive presses for making olive oil, a water well and rooms for storing olive oil. So we know Nazareth was a small farming village in Mary's time. Perhaps Mary came from a family of olive farmers.

DAY 6

A baby with
a throne

⊙ Where are we going today?
Teenager Mary is told by an angel that she will have a baby. That's not even the most surprising part of the story!

Pray: Dear Father, as we hear about the baby born at Christmas, please help us to hear the story as if for the first time. Amen.

❓ Ask a quick question
Can you think of something that lasts a long time? What animal lives the longest? What is the oldest item in our home? What sweet lasts longest?

Link: Today we are told that this baby will rule forever. "Forever" is very hard to understand.

Today's story
- *Where are we in the Bible?* We heard yesterday that God sent the angel Gabriel to the little village of Nazareth to speak to a young woman called Mary.

- *Look out for each detail we are told about Mary's baby.*

- *Read the passage. For young children, show them the picture and then draw the promises that the angel Gabriel makes; pregnant, a son, Jesus, a throne, a people. (Don't worry if you struggle with drawing—stick men are fine.)*

Luke 1 v 28-33
²⁸ *The angel came to [Mary] and said, "Greetings! The Lord has blessed you and is with you."*

²⁹ But Mary was very confused by what the angel said. Mary wondered, "What does this mean?"

³⁰ The angel said to her, "Don't be afraid, Mary, because God is pleased with you. ³¹ Listen! You will become pregnant. You will give birth to a son, and you will name him Jesus. ³² He will be great, and people will call him the Son of the Most High. The Lord God will give him the throne of King David, his ancestor. ³³ He will rule over the people of Jacob forever. His kingdom will never end."

Question for 3s and 4s

What did the angel say was going to happen to Mary? (*She was going to have a baby.*)

Question for 5-7s

What name was Mary told to give her baby? (*Read verse 31: "You will name him Jesus".*)

Question for over-7s

Look again at verse 33. What makes Jesus different to other kings and queens from history? (*Lots! Jesus is King for ever. So he doesn't need to go to war, because he is always in charge. He doesn't worry about his enemies, because he always wins. He is always incredibly powerful. And he can escape death unlike every other ruler.*)

Question for teens

Sometimes Christians get laughed at for trusting in a long-dead religious guy. When a Christian feels embarrassed for trusting in Jesus, what is there in today's announcement to remember? (*No matter what our friends think, Jesus Christ will be King forever. There will never be one moment when Jesus is beaten. And ultimately, every Christian will be found on the winning side under our eternal King.*)

Think and pray

Give thanks that we have a risen, ruling, forever King. Or pray for any Christians who feel weak, lonely and far from their mighty King.

Want to get dramatic?

Each time we meet the angel Gabriel, he says, "Don't be afraid", so he must have been frightening. God's messengers are more like terrifying warriors than frilly fairies. Can you dress up a child as the angel Gabriel? You could start with a white sheet and add some tin foil or toy armour and perhaps a cardboard helmet.

Got time to chat?

I don't want to be the Grinch, but nothing about Christmas lasts long. The Christmas tree will soon arrive and then go back. The presents are being wrapped in paper, which will soon go into the recycling. But we are celebrating the forever King—King Jesus. It is because he rose from the dead that we are celebrating his birth. How could we make sure that our family remembers that Jesus Christ will still be reigning when Christmas is finished?

Something more for the adults?

Drink in the promise of Isaiah 9 v 7 (NIV). See your King enthroned on high.

> *Of the greatness of his government and peace*
>   *there will be no end.*
> *He will reign on David's throne*
>   *and over his kingdom,*
> *establishing and upholding it*
>   *with justice and righteousness*
>   *from that time on and for ever.*
> *The zeal of the LORD Almighty*
>   *will accomplish this.*

Fun fact

A thousand years before Mary, God had promised King David that a son from his family would be king on his throne for ever. You can read about that in 2 Samuel 7 v 12-16.

A thousand years is a long time to wait for a promise to be kept. Imagine a promise made to us at the Battle of Hastings in 1066 that is finally kept today. Think about all those people who had to trust that one day God would keep his promise, but died without ever seeing that king.

DAY 7

How?

⊙ Where are we going today?
God placed his own Son into Mary's tummy. Mary trusted God.

Pray: Dear Father, thank you that you gave us your Son as a baby. Amen.

❓ Ask a quick question
Imagine walking into our kitchen on the morning of Christmas day and seeing something unbelievable waiting for you. What would make your mind explode? What would make you say, "How could this happen?"

Link: In today's story we hear Mary ask, "How could this happen?" because God's gift to her exploded her mind.

Today's story
- *Where are we in the Bible? The angel Gabriel has just promised Mary a son who will rule over God's people for ever. It's not surprising that she has a question for Gabriel.*

- *Look out for how the angel answers Mary's question.*

- *Read the passage. For young children, find two large, empty bottles to be Mary and Elizabeth. Place a marble, stone or raisin into each bottle when the angel explains that they will be pregnant.*

Luke 1 v 34-38
34 Mary said to the angel, "How will this happen? I am a virgin!"

35 The angel said to Mary, "The Holy Spirit will come upon you, and the power of the Most High will cover you. The baby will be holy. He will be called the Son of God. 36 Now listen! Elizabeth, your relative, is very old. But she is also pregnant with a son. Everyone thought she could not have a baby, but she has been pregnant for six months. 37 God can do everything!"

38 Mary said, "I am the servant girl of the Lord. Let this happen to me as you say!" Then the angel went away.

———————— **?** ————————

Question for 3s and 4s
What is the special present that God will give Mary?

Question for 5-7s
Mary's not the only one with a miracle baby! Who else is having one?

Question for over-7s
How is this going to happen? *(It's all right to go a bit hazy on the details. How does any miracle happen? The Holy Spirit will be with Mary in a special way to place the Son of God in Mary's tummy.)*

Question for teens
Mary's life was about to get turned upside down, not always in a good way. Read verse 38. Why would she say this? *(I don't think it's because this was great news. The months and years ahead would be full of risk and worry. But Mary trusted God and believed that his plan was the good one, even if it would hurt. That is faith.)*

Think and pray
Thank God that he really can do everything. What is the best thing he did in today's story?

! OPTIONAL EXTRAS

Want to get techy?
Can you find a film of what a baby inside a mum's tummy looks like?

Got time to chat?
Someone has said that FAITH means *Forgetting All I Trust Him*. Mary shows us what this looks like in today's story. Mary is about to become impossibly pregnant. She trusts God and believes that it will be all right, even in the midst of all the questions she must have: Will Joseph still want to marry her if she is pregnant? How will she cope when the whole village thinks she is lying about

being pregnant with God's baby? How can she be a good parent to God's own Son when she's never even had her own child before? In spite of all those questions, Mary trusts God.

Where is the worry, the fear, the nervousness or the confusion in your life? Can you trust God with it?

Something more for the adults?

While Mary is processing the full life-changing implications of this message, the angel concludes his bombshell announcement with these words: "For no word from God will ever fail" (v 37, NIV). In Mary's shoes, I might have quietly wished that there had been some sort of administrative error and actually these words would not come to pass after all. Not so Mary. She heard the Lord's words. She was certain that they would come pass. She knew she could depend on him through their fulfilment. And today, as you and I hear the words of God in the Bible, we can say with Mary, "May your word to me be fulfilled" (v 38, NIV).

DAY 8

A boy
named Joseph

⊙ Where are we going today?
Joseph was about to marry Mary, but he found out she was pregnant, so he decided to quietly break it off.

Pray: Dear Father, thank you that the first Christmas was a story of you using ordinary people and helping them to trust you. Help us to trust you too. Amen.

Ask a quick question
Can you think of a time when something surprising happened to you or your family, which meant you had to change your plans?

Link: Today we'll see that being pregnant with Jesus was a disaster for Mary and Joseph's plans.

Today's story
- *Where are we in the Bible?* We have been in Luke's Gospel hearing about Mary. We are jumping into Matthew's Gospel to hear about Joseph. Matthew is a different Gospel writer, interested in different people but telling us the same story of Jesus' birth.

- *Look out for* Joseph changing his plans.

- *Read the passage.* For young children, grab two toy figures (or two people) to show the stages in the story: Mary > Joseph > join to be married > Mary pregnant > Joseph plans to separate.

Matthew 1 v 18-19
[18] *The mother of Jesus Christ was Mary. And this is how the birth of Jesus came about. Mary was engaged to marry Joseph. But before they married, she learned that she was going to have a baby. She was*

*pregnant by the power of the Holy Spirit. ¹⁹ Mary's husband, Joseph, was
a good man. He did not want to disgrace her in public, so he planned to
divorce her secretly.*

?

Question for 3s and 4s

What was Mary's big news? *(Mary was going to have a baby.)*

Question for 5-7s

Joseph had a big problem. What had he and Mary been planning to do?
*(Mary and Joseph were about to get married. Joseph found out Mary was
pregnant, but he knew he wasn't the father of the baby.)*

Question for over-7s

How did Joseph work out what to do next? *(He decided he couldn't marry
Mary because she was pregnant with another man's baby—or so he thought!
But Joseph was a good, kind man, so he didn't want to make a big thing of
the divorce. Being pregnant with a baby that didn't belong to Joseph was
already going to ruin Mary's life, and Joseph's, but he didn't want to make
it worse.)*

Question for teens

What do you think of Joseph's plan? What would you have done? *(Jewish laws
said that a woman should be punished for getting pregnant with a man who
wasn't her husband. If Joseph married Mary, it would have looked like he
was to blame. At least Joseph was trying to look after Mary by breaking up
quietly. There were no winners.)*

Think and pray

Dear Father, thank you for helping us to trust you when our plans don't work
out. Amen.

! OPTIONAL EXTRAS

Want to get laughing?
Can you make up unbelievable excuses for what has happened to you? For example, "I'm sorry I'm so muddy but a huge digger dumped its load on me as I walked past."

Got time to chat?
Messy lives don't always mean that we have got something wrong. Joseph hadn't done anything wrong. He was a good man, trying to make good decisions. We know that God's hand was in it. We know how this mess was turned into something beautiful. This is the normal story of trusting God. Our messy lives, our love for others and our godly choices are being used by God to make something beautiful. What is messy in your life at the moment?

Something more for the adults?
Read Deuteronomy 22 v 22-24. Imagine Joseph reading these words as he tried to find a way through this. By the 1st century, people may no longer have been stoned for breaking God's law, but this was still the cultural background and the basis of Joseph's decision-making. If Joseph took Mary as his wife, then their community would assume that they hadn't waited—which would mean public disgrace. If Joseph broke off the engagement, then their community would turn on Mary—also public disgrace. Some decisions feel like a dead weight on top of us. There doesn't appear to be any good outcome. This is why we must trust God.

DAY 9

He will save us

⊙ Where are we going today?
An angel told Joseph that Mary's baby was going to save his people.

Pray: Dear Father, help us to understand how we can be saved by Mary's baby. Amen.

❓ Ask a quick question
Think of some people whose job it is to save others. How many jobs can you think of?

Link: Today we're seeing that all of us need the baby in Mary's tummy to save us.

Today's story
- *Where are we in the Bible?* Joseph and Mary were engaged to be married. Suddenly Mary was pregnant and Joseph was sure he wasn't the father, so he decided to quietly tell Mary that he didn't want to marry her anymore.

- *Look out for* what Joseph finds out about Mary's baby.

- *Read the passage. For young children, get out paper and a pen to draw the angel's message using very simple stick figures and shapes. (For instance, draw a crown in the air for "the Holy Spirit", a life ring for "save" and a squiggly mess for "sins".)*

Matthew 1 v 20-21
[20] *While Joseph thought about this, an angel of the Lord came to him in a dream. The angel said, "Joseph, descendant of David, don't be afraid to take Mary as your wife. The baby in her is from the Holy Spirit.* [21] *She will give birth to a son. You will name the son Jesus. Give him that name because he will save his people from their sins."*

?

Question for 3s and 4s

Who told Joseph all about Mary's baby?

Question for 5-7s

What was Joseph told about the baby in Mary's tummy?

Question for over-7s

What was the baby born to do? How do you think it feels to be saved? (*The name "Jesus" means "God saves". Jesus was born to save his people from their sins. We often don't feel as if we need saving from our sins, but Jesus came to do just that. When we're saved, we are safe; we are not in danger anymore and we can stop worrying. How does that make you feel? Relieved, pleased, thankful or amazed?*)

Question for teens

Not everyone thinks they need saving. Often people think to themselves, "I'm sure I've done enough to make God love me." What kinds of things do people do to make them feel like they've done enough? (*Some people try to be really good, by being kind to others and being the best they can be. Some people dedicate their whole lives to doing good—in many ways, their lives look better than ours! Others think of their religion as being like a magic token to exchange for their god's love. Maybe you thought of other ways as well. Have they done enough?*)

Think and pray

Thank Jesus that he was born to save you, to make you one of his people, and to give you the chance to know you are safe in God's family.

Want to get baking?

Make donut life rings. Buy some plain ring donuts. Make some red and white icing by mixing icing sugar with a little water and a few drops of food colouring. Colour alternate quarters of the donuts with the red and white icing to make them look like swimming-pool life rings. Who uses one of these to save others? How did Jesus save us?

Got time to chat?

If we live thinking we can save ourselves, then every day can be a series of thrilling highs and miserable lows—the highs when we feel like we've done enough and the lows when we feel like we've blown it. Have you had a low or a high today? In a low, you can talk about why Jesus was born to do what we can't do for ourselves. In a high, you can talk about the best high of knowing he has done it all for us.

Something more for the adults?

"Don't be afraid to take Mary as your wife." Joseph was asked to join Mary in the disgrace that was heading towards her. Jesus' birth did not fit with their culture's norms. Jesus brought disgrace. Jesus still brings disgrace on his followers. Living for Jesus means we will not fit with our culture's norms. Hear the angel's words, "Don't be afraid". Continue to be brave, accepting disgrace, knowing that Jesus is delighted with you.

DAY 10

God with us

⊙ Where are we going today?
Jesus is God himself, come to live with ordinary people like us.

Pray: Dear Father, we don't just want to learn more about Jesus—we want to be ruled by him. Please help us. Amen.

? Ask a quick question
Pick someone in our family. In what ways are they different to you? In what ways are they the same as you?

Link: Today we're seeing that Jesus looked ordinary, but he was totally different to every other person.

Today's story
- *Where are we in the Bible?* Joseph has had a life-changing dream. Next, Matthew explains that long ago a prophet had promised and explained all this.

- *Look out for* what Joseph decided to do next.

- *Read the passage. For young children, you could write out the prophecy (v 23) on a piece of paper; then put it in an envelope to open and read out at the right moment, to show it is a message from God delivered long ago.*

Matthew 1 v 22-25
²² All this happened to make clear the full meaning of what the Lord had said through the prophet: ²³ "The virgin will be pregnant. She will have a son, and they will name him Immanuel." This name means "God is with us." ²⁴ When Joseph woke up, he did what the Lord's angel had told him to do. Joseph married Mary. ²⁵ But he did not have intimate relations with her until she gave birth to the son. And Joseph named the son Jesus.

?

Question for 3s and 4s

After Joseph woke up, what did he decide to do next?

Question for 5-7s

God had promised long ago that a young woman would have a baby who people would call *Immanuel*. Did you hear what *Immanuel* means?

Question for over-7s

If this promised baby is really "God with us", can you think of two ways in which he will be different to every other person who has ever lived? *(Jesus is different to us in all the ways God is different to us. Jesus could create just by speaking (John 2 v 1-10), he knew everything about people he met (John 4 v 17-19), he was perfectly good, and... The list is long!)*

Question for teens

Jesus is "God with us". He became just like you and experienced what it's like to be human. How would you finish this sentence? "It's strange to think that Jesus also knows what it's like to..." *(Jesus knows what it feels like to be bullied, to be alone, to be exhausted, to be overwhelmed with sadness and worry. Jesus was let down by friends and laughed at. He also became our sin (2 Corinthians 5 v 21), so he understands our shame. Don't forget that he also went to parties, laughed, loved, was loved—and maybe he was embarrassed by his dad's dancing!)*

 Think and pray

Thank Jesus for who he is and tell him what you need (because he can help!).

! OPTIONAL EXTRAS

Want to get baking?

Make some gingerbread men, or any people-shaped biscuits. God became one of us—really like us, really with us. He understands us.

Got time to chat?

Are we living as though Jesus is God? Because if he is God, then there is no worry, no habit, no behaviour, and no illness that he can't help us with. Think of the biggest problem facing you today, and take it to Jesus, who is God with us.

Something more for the adults?

John Wesley was a leader in the 18th-century revival in England. We read this about the final moments of his life: "Finding [his friends] could not understand what he said, he paused a little, and then with all the remaining strength he had, cried out, 'The best of all is, God is with us'." "God with us" gives us plenty to dwell on in our minds and hearts this Christmas. If God went to such trouble to be with us, how can we ensure this Christmas that we remain in him?

DAY 11

Leaping for joy

⊙ Where are we going today?

While Jesus was in Mary's tummy, he made John leap for joy in Elizabeth's tummy.

Pray: Dear Father, please help us to leap for joy as we get to know Jesus better. Amen.

❓ Ask a quick question

Does anything make you leap for joy, punch the air, and shout, "Yes!"?

Link: Today we see Jesus made people leap for joy, before he was even born!

Today's story

- *Where are we in the Bible?* The angel Gabriel told Mary that her elderly relative Elizabeth was having a baby too. As soon as the angel left, Mary headed off on the long journey to see Elizabeth.

- *Look out for who is very happy in this story.*

- *Read the passage. For young children, read only the **bold** text. Do two of you feel like sticking cushions up your shirts to act out Mary and Elizabeth?*

Luke 1 v 39-45

39 Mary got up and went quickly to a town in the mountains of Judea. 40 She went to Zechariah's house and greeted Elizabeth. 41 When Elizabeth heard Mary's greeting, the unborn baby inside Elizabeth jumped. Then Elizabeth was filled with the Holy Spirit. 42 She cried out in a loud voice, "God has blessed you more than any other woman. And God has blessed the baby which you will give birth to. 43 You are the mother of my Lord, and you have come to me! Why has something so *good happened to me?* **⁴⁴ When I heard your voice, the baby inside me jumped with joy. ⁴⁵ You are blessed because you believed what the Lord said to you would really happen."**

———————————— **?** ————————————

Question for 3s and 4s

What did John do in Elizabeth's tummy when Elizabeth met Mary?

Question for 5-7s

Who is happy in this story? (*Elizabeth is happy. The baby John is happy. Mary is happy too! "Blessed" means "happy".*)

Question for over-7s

Can you see *why* Elizabeth and the baby in her tummy were happy? If you can answer that, then you can grab a slice of that joy for yourself! (*John was joyful in Elizabeth's tummy to meet Jesus in Mary's tummy. And Elizabeth was happy to meet the mother of Jesus (v 43). We can find joy by meeting Jesus too, as we read the Bible.*)

Question for teens

We all want to be happy. "Blessed" is a Bible word for when God gives us a deep, deep happiness that lasts and lasts. Look at verse 45. What did Mary do that made her blessed? How can you experience this blessing too? *Elizabeth tells Mary: "You are blessed because you believed what the Lord said to you would really happen." We will be blessed if we believe God's promises to us in the Bible. Will we believe that the greatest, deepest happiness comes from trusting God?*

Think and pray

What makes you leap for joy? Thank God for that thing, and for the fact that the joy that Jesus gives us never goes away.

! OPTIONAL EXTRAS

Want to get busy?

Do you have a Christian friend who makes you happy when you are together, like Mary and Elizabeth? Send them a message saying, "You make me happy. Thank you!" or write them a card saying, "Keep trusting Jesus with me!"

Got time to chat?

What does your family want more of? We want more of something if we think it will make us happy. If we think stuff will make us happy, we want more money. If we think sugar will make us happy, we want more sweets. If we think friends will make us happy, we want more of those too. This story teaches us that trusting God's promises is what will make us truly happy (blessed)—so what we should really want is more faith!

Something more for the adults?

Read Luke 1 v 46-56. (We're not doing these verses with the children, but you can enjoy them. Perhaps if something strikes you, you can share it with your child later.) God brings down the proud and lifts up the weak and humble. As a parent, it is tempting to want to always appear in control, to always have the right answers, and to have enough of everything to provide for our children. What would it look like for your child to sometimes see you hungry, humble and fearful before God?

DAY 12

Off to Bethlehem

⊙ Where are we going today?

The most powerful person in the world at that time sent Mary and Joseph to Bethlehem—which was exactly what God had planned.

Pray: Dear Father, please show us that you are in charge, even when it doesn't look like it. Amen.

❓ Ask a quick question

Who are the most powerful people you have ever heard of? Who is in charge of places you go to?

Link: Today we're meeting the most powerful person in the world at the time Jesus was born.

Today's story

- *Where are we in the Bible?* The year is about 3 or 4 BC: more than 2,000 years ago. Mary is pregnant with Jesus, about to be married to Joseph, and living in the small town of Nazareth.

- *Look out for* why Mary and Joseph had to travel a long way.

- *Read the passage.* For young children, start reading in one room and then walk to another part of your home when Mary and Joseph travel in verse 4.

Luke 2 v 1-5

¹ At that time, Augustus Caesar sent an order to all people in the countries that were under Roman rule. The order said that they must list their names in a register. ² This was the first registration taken while Quirinius was governor of Syria. ³ And everyone went to their own towns to be registered.

⁴ So Joseph left Nazareth, a town in Galilee. He went to the town of Bethlehem in Judea. This town was known as the town of David. Joseph went there because he was from the family of David. ⁵ Joseph registered with Mary because she was engaged to marry him. (Mary was now pregnant.)

Question for 3s and 4s
Where did Mary and Joseph have to travel to?

Question for 5-7s
Why did they have to go there?

Question for over-7s
Who *seemed* to be in charge in this story? Who was *really* in charge? *(The Roman emperor, Augustus Caesar, was the most powerful man in the world. His command sent Mary and Joseph to Bethlehem, King David's town. But hundreds of years earlier God had promised that his ruler would be born there (Micah 5 v 2). God was perfectly in charge, even using the Roman emperor for his plans!)*

Question for teens
God used the Roman emperor to send a heavily pregnant teenager and her fiancé off on a 90-mile journey far from home. What comfort is there for us when those in authority make life harder for Christians? *(God has promised that he is in charge of every detail, so the Christian can be sure that God is working out his good plans, even when things seem to be getting harder (Romans 8 v 28). We don't need to rule the world because God already does.)*

Think and pray
Thank God that he is in charge of every little detail, even when it feels very hard. Pray about a hard part of your life, asking God to help you trust him in it.

! OPTIONAL EXTRAS

Want to get techy?
Using Google Maps or a similar satnav app, find a route to walk the journey from Nazareth to Bethlehem. How long would it take to walk?

Got time to chat?

Think of a situation where someone else's decision is making your life harder. How could God use that decision for your good, making you more like Jesus?

Something more for the adults?

Martin Luther was a key figure in the Reformation in the 16th century—a movement which rediscovered the glory of the gospel after it had become hidden under religion and tradition. Luther spent much of his life hiding and fighting against the authorities. He used to say to his anxious friend, Philip, *Stop trying to govern the world.*[1] Leave the governing of the world to the Lord! He will send relief and help at just the right time. He is ruling and knows better than we do what we need. In what parts of your life are you trying to "govern the world"?

Fun fact

Augustus Caesar was one of the best emperors the Roman Empire had. He built a great network of roads, and introduced early forms of fire brigade, police force and postal service. By the time he died, he ruled over most of Europe and the lands all around the Mediterranean. Many statues of him survive today. We even know that he had gaps in his teeth and curly hair and that his eyebrows met in the middle! Can you find a picture of him in a book or online?

---

1 J.C. Ryle, *Expository Thoughts on the Gospels: Gospel of Luke, Volume 2* (The Banner of Truth Trust, 1997), p 50. Actual quote, "Cease, Philip, to try to govern the world."

The big birth

⊙ Where are we going today?

Jesus was born! His arrival into our world was hard.

Pray: Dear Father, help us to hear how Jesus was born into our world. Amen.

❓ Ask a quick question

How would you know if you were seeing a royal birth? What do you think is different about the birth of a king or queen compared to your birth or mine?

Link: Today we see how the greatest king was born. It's not what you expect!

Today's story

- *Where are we in the Bible?* Mary and Joseph have arrived in Bethlehem to register after the Roman emperor ordered everyone to go to the town where their family came from.

- *Look out for* the different problems Mary and Joseph had.

- *Read the passage.* For young children, you could wrap a doll in cloths and place it in a rough box as you read the story.

Luke 2 v 6-7

⁶ *While Joseph and Mary were in Bethlehem, the time came for her to have the baby.* ⁷ *She gave birth to her first son. There were no rooms left in the inn. So she wrapped the baby with cloths and laid him in a box where animals are fed.*

---------- **?** ----------

Question for 3s and 4s

Where did they put Jesus when he was born?

Question for 5-7s

What problems did Mary and Joseph have in today's story?

Question for over-7s

How would the moment of Jesus' birth have felt for Mary, do you think? Is this different to the kinds of pictures we see on Christmas cards and in paintings? *(Mary gave birth. Having a baby is a shouty, painful, frightening business, so Mary must have been pretty flustered. This was a real couple, alone, in a real room, giving birth to a real baby.)*

Question for teens

If Jesus Christ arrived in the midst of poverty and rejection, how should that change his followers' choices?

 Think and pray

Thank Jesus that he chose a manger, not a palace, when he came to earth.

! OPTIONAL EXTRAS

Want to get crafty?

Make a Christmas card with a manger (an animal's feeding box) on it. You could use lollypop sticks or twigs for the manger and kitchen roll for strips of linen. What message could you write inside the card to tell someone about the most exciting part of Christmas? Who will you send it to? Can you think of someone who might be finding Christmas difficult, like Mary and Joseph?

Got time to chat?

Jesus' birth shows that we're making a mistake if we make decisions about others based on what they look like. How do you feel when you see the poorest or the weakest in your community? Could we do anything this Christmas to show them respect and care?

Something more for the adults?

John 1 v 14 says, "The Word became flesh and made his dwelling among us" (NIV).

The eternal, all-powerful Word came to make his home next door to you. He breathed your air. He drank your water. He made himself right at home. Even though he did not belong, he chose to stay—he is still human in heaven today. Jesus is no distant dictator behind a high wall. He is your neighbour.

DAY 14

Burning up the night

⊙ Where are we going today?
The angels told the shepherds that the birth of Jesus was the best news possible.

Pray: Dear Father, please help us share the shepherds' amazement at the birth of the baby Jesus. Amen.

❓ Ask a quick question
What would be good news, bringing joy to everyone who lives on our road?

Link: Today we're finding out what would be good news bringing joy to all people.

Today's story
- *Where are we in the Bible?* When Jesus was born in Bethlehem, he was laid in an animal's feeding trough. Meanwhile on the hills, in the darkness, outside Bethlehem…

- *Look out for* who the angel says this baby is.

- *Read the passage. For young children, tell this story under a blanket and turn on a lamp or torch at the right moment.*

Luke 2 v 8-12
[8] That night, some shepherds were in the fields nearby watching their sheep. [9] An angel of the Lord stood before them. The glory of the Lord was shining around them, and suddenly they became very frightened. [10] The angel said to them, "Don't be afraid, because I am bringing you some good news. It will be a joy to all the people. [11] Today your Saviour was born in David's town. He is Christ, the Lord. [12] This is how you will know him: You will find a baby wrapped in cloths and lying in a feeding box."

?

Question for 3s and 4s
Who came to visit the shepherds?

Question for 5-7s
Who did the angel say had been born in Bethlehem? What did the angel tell the shepherds to look out for, so they could find him?

Question for over-7s
Jesus' birth was the biggest news any human had ever heard! Why do you think God chose some clueless shepherds to be the first to hear it? Who would you have chosen to tell first? (*Perhaps we'd tell the most powerful, the most wealthy or the most famous people. God chose to tell shepherds to show that the Saviour had come for normal people, like you and me.*)

Question for teens
Which of these do you think is the hardest to believe, and why?

- That an angel would be sent to announce such big news to dirty shepherds in a field

- That this baby could be good news for absolutely all people

- That an angel actually appeared

- That all of us need rescuing

Think and pray
Thank God for one surprise from today's story.

A note about Christ

"Christ" is the King that God had been promising his people for hundreds of years, who would rescue them and rule for ever. What a King he would be! And what a long time they had been waiting for him.

! OPTIONAL EXTRAS

Want to get dramatic?
One of you pretend to be the angel, while the rest pretend to be the shepherds, sitting by your fire on the hillside, taking about sheep, the weather and plans for the weekend. Then the angel steps out and the shepherds need to be as shocked as it's possible to be. Can you give the angel's message in your own words?

Got time to chat?
There isn't much good news on the news. Have you noticed? It's hard to catch any really good news, let alone good news for everyone. What good news for the world would make it into the news?

Something more for the adults?
Read Romans 1 v 16-17. The gospel message is such good news of great joy for all people that Paul is not ashamed of it. When we come across such wildly good news, we want to tell everyone because it is good news for them. Our decision to tell others about Jesus Christ has to start with a deep, deep certainty that what we are telling them is good news for them that will bring them great joy.

DAY 15

Turn up
the music

⊙ Where are we going today?
Jesus' birth caused a whole army of angels to sing to God for bringing us peace.

Pray: Dear Father, thank you that the army of angels came out to sing to you when Jesus was born. Please give us hearts full of praise. Amen.

Ask a quick question
Has anyone ever stopped being your friend? Do you remember how it felt?

Link: Today's story is an ear-bursting celebration of a friendship being mended.

Today's story
- *Where are we in the Bible?* An angel appeared to the shepherds and half-blinded them with his glory. Imagine what a whole army of angels would do to them!

- *Look out for* what these angels wanted to sing about.

- *Read the passage. For young children, sing the angels' song together at least three times.*

Luke 2 v 13-14
*¹³ Then a very large group of angels from heaven joined the first angel.
All the angels were praising God, saying: ¹⁴ "Give glory to God in heaven,
and on earth let there be peace to the people who please God."*

?

Question for 3s and 4s

Pretend to be one of the army of singing angels. Can you do these actions as I say them? "God is amazing. He makes my feet jump, my mouth sing, my arms wave, my hands clap and my heart beat. The almighty God is making peace with you! Let's jump, shout and sing to him until we can't sing anymore."

Question for 5-7s

If you had been a shepherd, what would you have done? Would you have hidden behind the other shepherds or stood and joined in?

Question for over-7s

Close your eyes and imagine what it would have been like as the angels sang, *Thank you God for this baby. He makes it possible for people to have peace with you.* Why is this good news? *(Before Jesus came, we were at war with God. Now with Jesus, there can be peace, joy and love.)*

Question for teens

Would anything make your heart explode with complete joy and wonder? What about the angel's message?

Think and pray

Give thanks to God for what you love most about him.

A note about glory

"Glory" is when God's brilliance can be seen in blinding, bright, powerful light. "Glory to God" is what to shout when you think God is absolutely, awesomely ace. We want everyone to know that all that power and wonder belongs to him.

! OPTIONAL EXTRAS

Want to get singing?
Play a song you all know on a device. Sing along all together. Then turn the volume down while you all keep singing. When you turn it up again, are you in the right place? Jesus is the best reason to sing.

Got time to chat?
When do you sing? What does it take to get you singing? If we truly understood what Jesus was like, we would sing all the time. Our hearts would be full of praise.

Something more for the adults?
How do you want to praise God? Sing it out to him? Pray it out with a smile? Open the door and shout it to the wind? Choose one way of praising God for who he is and what he did that first Christmas, for you. Join the army of angels in bringing glory to God today.

DAY 16

See
the baby

📍 **Where are we going today?**
The shepherds rushed to find the Saviour baby exactly as the angel had told them.

Pray: Dear Father, please help us to feel some of the shepherd's excitement as they saw our King for the first time. Amen.

❓ **Ask a quick question**
Can you describe exactly where you are sitting now so that someone else could find you?

Link: In today's story, the shepherds went to look for the baby—exactly as the angel had told them to.

Today's story

- *Where are we in the Bible?* The full army of angels has just filled the hills with worship. What's next for the shepherds?

- *Look out for* what the shepherds find.

- *Read the passage. For young children, hide a baby doll. Read the passage as you look for him; and then find him just at the right moment.*

Luke 2 v 15-17a

¹⁵ Then the angels left the shepherds and went back to heaven. The shepherds said to each other, "Let us go to Bethlehem and see this thing that has happened. We will see this thing the Lord told us about."

¹⁶ So the shepherds went quickly and found Mary and Joseph. ¹⁷ And the shepherds saw the baby lying in a feeding box.

?

Question for 3s and 4s
What did the shepherds want to do as soon as the angels left?

Question for 5-7s
Look at the picture of the moment when the shepherds found the baby, exactly as the angel described (p 64). What do you think the shepherds would have whispered to each other as they looked into the manger?

Question for over-7s
These shepherds were super-ordinary, with mud caked into their fingers, dust in their matted hair and scars on their arms from their work. What do you think they would remember most about that night? What questions do you think they left with? (*What a night! I think they may have left asking, "When do you think we'll next hear about him? Will it be when he is crowned? Or maybe when he moves into his palace?"*)

Question for teens
See the picture of the shepherds looking at the baby (p 64). This is the baby who the angel promised would be your Saviour, your long-promised King and your Lord. What do you think as you look at the picture? Would you have hoped for something more than an ordinary baby? (*We can trust Jesus, not because of what he looks like but because of what the angel said: "Your Saviour was born in David's town. He is Christ, the Lord."*)

Think and pray
Thank God that the baby sent to rescue and to rule was real: real enough for the shepherds to see and touch and even smell.

Want to get baking?
Ice a biscuit and scatter some broken-up shredded wheat (or other breakfast cereal) over the top, as hay in the manger. Lay a jelly baby on the hay.

Got time to chat?
Would it make it easier for us to trust Jesus if that amazing evening had happened to us instead of the shepherds? Remember, this is the reason why Luke spoke to the eyewitnesses: so that we could be certain of these things. This first Christmas did happen. Luke might have met one or more of these shepherds. What do you think the shepherds would have told Luke?

Something more for the adults?
Read John 1 v 1-5. Imagine this as the words of the shepherds. Meditate on these words. What is your response to the shepherds' discovery?

DAY 17

Sharing the story

⊙ Where are we going today?

Jesus' birth was so thrilling that the shepherds told everyone the good news about this baby and shouted thanks to God.

Pray: Dear Father, please help us to praise and thank you as the shepherds did. Amen.

❓ Ask a quick question

What would make you knock on every door in our road?

Link: We're going see that the shepherds wanted to knock on every door in the whole town!

Today's story

- *Where are we in the Bible?* The shepherds heard from the angel who the baby was and how they would know they had found him. They ran to look for him. They found him. They were thrilled to meet their Saviour.

- *Look out for* what the shepherds did next.

- *Read the passage. For young children, use toy figures (or spice jars) for Mary, for the shepherds and for the people the shepherds told. Mary stayed with Jesus. The shepherds ran through Bethlehem and ended up with their sheep in the hills. Tell the story of this journey as you read.*

Luke 2 v 17b-20

17b Then [the shepherds] told what the angels had said about this child. 18 Everyone was amazed when they heard what the shepherds said to them. 19 Mary hid these things in her heart; she continued to think about them. 20 Then the shepherds went back to their sheep, praising God and thanking him for everything that they had seen and heard. It was just as the angel had told them.

———————— **?** ————————

Question for 3s and 4s

So what did the shepherds do next? What are they doing in the pictures (p 67)?

Question for 5-7s

What made these shepherds want to wake up the town with the news, and then sing and shout in the dark, in the middle of a field of sheep? *(They felt like they had just won every prize in every competition all at once. They had met the forever King of the world.)*

Question for over-7s

What do you think the shepherds shouted as they ran down the street?

Question for teens

"Mary hid these things in her heart; she continued to think about them." Mary responded quite differently from the shepherds. How do you think she was feeling? What do you think she was thinking about? *(Although Mary had an angel visit her, it must still have been a shock when shepherds she'd never met burst into her barn with their story! It's worth thinking deeply with Mary about exactly who this baby was.)*

————————————————————

Think and pray

Pray for the Spirit to give you the same thrill and excitement as the shepherds. Or thank God for the opportunities you have this Christmas to tell others about Jesus, as the shepherds did.

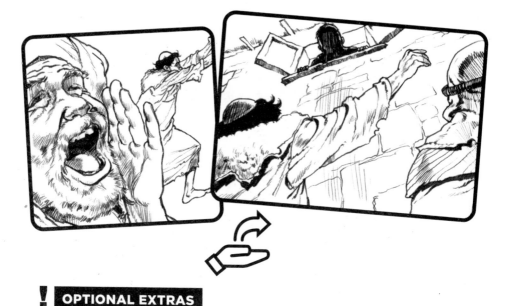

⚠ OPTIONAL EXTRAS

Want to get techy?
Create a one-minute film on a phone to tell the world about this baby. What have you learned from the story so far? What do your viewers need to know?

Got time to chat?
The shepherds are different from us in so many ways. They lived a long time ago. They were shepherds. They met angels. They talked to Mary and Joseph. They met Jesus in the flesh. But what could be the *same* about the shepherds and us?

Something more for the adults?
What is there here to hide in your heart: to continue to think about? You can have questions. You don't need to know all the answers. Just like Mary, we are being used by the Lord for his glory, but we don't need to know exactly how the Lord will use our fresh understanding of his Son. God has told us what we need to know. We are safe. While we wait for God's purposes to be revealed on the day Jesus returns, we can ponder the truth that he has shown us.

A promise kept

⊙ Where are we going today?

Simeon knew that the baby was the world's promised rescuer.

Pray: Dear Father, please help us to understand why Simeon was so happy that he felt ready to die. Amen.

Ask a quick question

What are you waiting for at the moment? Is there something that you really wish could happen today?

Link: We're going to meet Simeon, who had spent his whole life waiting for God to show him his rescuing King.

Today's story

- *Where are we in the Bible?* Mary and Joseph have gone to Jerusalem, to the temple, to offer a gift to God for their son and to have him named.

- *Look out for* what Simeon says.

- *Read the passage. For young children, pretend to be the old man Simeon, telling your child all about yourself, or let your child play the part of Simeon. Stop reading at the end of verse 30.*

Luke 2 v 25-33

25 A man named Simeon lived in Jerusalem. He was a good man and very religious. He was waiting for the time when God would help Israel. The Holy Spirit was in him. 26 The Holy Spirit told Simeon that he would not die before he saw the Christ promised by the Lord. 27 The Spirit led Simeon to the Temple. Mary and Joseph brought the baby Jesus to the Temple to do what the law said they must do. 28 Then Simeon took the baby in his arms and thanked God:

²⁹ "Now, Lord, you can let me, your servant,
   die in peace as you said.
³⁰ I have seen your Salvation with my own eyes.
   ³¹ You prepared him before all people.
³² He is a light for the non-Jewish people to see.
   He will bring honour to your people, the Israelites."

³³ Jesus' father and mother were amazed at what Simeon had said about him.

Question for 3s and 4s
What did Simeon do with the baby Jesus?

Question for 5-7s
What had Simeon been waiting for? *(He had been waiting for the time when God would help Israel (v 25). God had promised Simeon that he would not die before he met this baby who would save God's people.)*

Question for over-7s
Look again at verse 29. Imagine waiting for something so precious that when you get it, you are happy to die! Simeon said that was his story. What had he got that was so precious? *(One old man, holding one tiny baby: a baby who was the only hope of rescue, not just for God's people, the Jews, but for every human who would ever live. What a moment!)*

Question for teens
We're all waiting for something. What are you waiting for? Does trusting God help you to wait with hope? *(Christians believe that Jesus will return, not in secret but in glorious, global visibility. Then, all waiting will be over. Until then, we wait for Christ's return, and he holds our longings in his care.)*

 Think and pray
What did Simeon teach you about Jesus? What was he certain about? Thank God for that.

❗ OPTIONAL EXTRAS

Want to get baking?

Growing up, my mum would say, "Wait and see" when I was over-excited about pudding. Which dessert teaches your family to wait with hope? If you want my suggestion, do a search for "self-saucing chocolate pudding"!

Got time to chat?

Waiting for Christmas is very difficult for the youngest members of our families. As our children get older, there are often harder, more painful reasons to wait—perhaps as they wait on God for him to bring them peace. If Christ is truly on his throne and he loves us, what could he be doing by making us wait like this, when it hurts so much?

Something more for the adults?

Read Luke 2 v 34-35. After Simeon has cradled Mary's precious son in his arms and said her baby will bring light to the world, he then casts a shadow over the next three decades of her family's life. Obedience to the light of the world was always costly and continues to be. How is it costly for you?

DAY 19

A very focused widow

⊙ Where are we going today?

Anna celebrated the fact that God had kept his greatest promise after she had waited a long time.

Pray: Dear Father, let us share Anna's overflowing excitement about Jesus' birth. Amen.

Ask a quick question

What do you think you are more focused on than anything else? What gets the best of your time?

Link: Today we meet Anna, who was in the temple every single day, missing meals and totally focused.

Today's story

- *Where are we in the Bible?* Mary and Joseph have taken the baby Jesus to the Temple in Jerusalem. An old man they have never met before tells them their baby will be a light for all. Then an old woman joins in with equal excitement!

- *Look out for what gets Anna most excited.*

- *Read the passage. For young children, tell the first half of the story to the middle of verse 37. Pause. Then ask your child how they think Anna felt (expecting them to say, "sad", "lonely" or "unhappy"). Then change the mood to be upbeat as you finish reading the story.*

Luke 2 v 36-38

[36] *Anna, a prophetess, was there at the Temple. She was from the family of Phanuel in the tribe of Asher. Anna was very old. She had once been*

married for seven years. [37] Then her husband died and she lived alone. She was now 84 years old. Anna never left the Temple. She worshipped God by going without food and praying day and night. [38] She was standing there [with Mary, Joseph and Simeon] at that time, thanking God. She talked about Jesus to all who were waiting for God to free Jerusalem.

———————————— **?** ————————————

Question for 3s and 4s

Look at the picture (p 73). Can you spot Mary and Joseph? Can you guess which of the others are Anna and Simeon? Why are they so happy?

Question for 5-7s

Anna met Jesus, Mary, Joseph and Simeon (v 38). She was so excited. What got Anna *most* excited that first Christmas?

Question for over-7s

Anna had waited for God to keep his promises. Then she saw the baby—God's promise kept. Are there any promises that you are still waiting for God to keep? Can you wait like Anna did? *(We're waiting for Jesus to come back to fix all that is broken. You might have thought of other promises as well. We can learn to wait like Anna: never losing hope, focusing on God, praying and worshipping with others. We can do all those things with our church as we wait together.)*

Question for teens

This keeps happening in Luke's story. Someone without power, who doesn't look much, who most people would ignore, finds out who this baby is, gets incredibly excited and then tells everyone they can. Why doesn't this seem to happen to the powerful, the rich and the popular? *(Anna worshipped God because she knew she was not the centre of the universe. Power, money, beauty and popularity all tempt us to believe that we are the centre of the universe. In the Bible it is normally the weak and the unimportant who trust God.)*

———————————————————————————

Think and pray

Anna spent her life thanking God and praying. Come up with three things each to thank God for. Anything. Fire out thank-you prayers. Get excited!

Want to get worshipping?

Anna spent her life worshipping. Take a moment to do that too. Worship God with prayer, with song or with an act of service. Pick it. Do it. With joy!

Got time to chat?

Sometimes it feels as if people "grow out" of Jesus, as you might grow out of a pair of jeans or you grow out of kids' films. What do you think Anna and Simeon might say to someone who thought they were just getting a bit too old for Jesus?

Something more for the adults?

There is something beautiful and inspiring about older Christians who model steady, godly passion for Jesus Christ. Do you have some people in your life like that? They need prayer and encouragement like the rest of us. Pray for them, asking that they would only keep growing in their love for Christ. What is your prayer for yourself for the next ten years? How would you like God change you?

A note about "waiting for God to free Jerusalem"

This means that they were waiting for God to send his final King to save his people. Anna knew that this promised King would come and take his people out of their pain and rule over them for a better future. That promise is for us too. We can get even more excited than Anna as we know how Jesus became that promised King.

DAY 20

Men from the east

 Where are we going today?

A group of very clever people came from far, far away to find Jesus and to worship him.

Pray: Dear Father, show us that anyone can worship Jesus this Christmas. Amen.

Ask a quick question

How far will you travel this Christmas?

Link: Today we're meeting people who had probably been travelling for more than a month to get to Jesus.

Today's story

- *Where are we in the Bible?* We are back in Matthew's Gospel. He tells us different parts of the story to Luke.

- *Look out for* who came looking for Jesus.

- *Read the passage.* For young children, can you find enough toy figures to show the wise men riding into a town to ask their questions?

Matthew 2 v 1-3

¹ Jesus was born in the town of Bethlehem in Judea during the time when Herod was king. After Jesus was born, some wise men from the east came to Jerusalem. ² They asked, "Where is the baby who was born to be the king of the Jews? We saw his star in the east. We came to worship him."

³ When King Herod heard about this new king of the Jews, he was troubled. And all the people in Jerusalem were worried too.

--- ? ---

Question for 3s and 4s

Who came looking for Jesus?

Question for 5-7s

Who did they say they were looking for? What did they want to do when they found him?

Question for over-7s

The wise men had travelled hundreds of miles. What made them go to all that trouble? What do you think they were expecting to find? *(They came because a new star had appeared. They had studied ancient books and prophecies to understand what it meant. The Holy Spirit must have been at work in them. They went to Jerusalem expecting the new king to be in the capital city, perhaps in gold robes, in a vast palace and surrounded by servants.)*

Question for teens

Some people say things like "You're only a Christian because you live in this country. You'd be a Hindu if you had grown up in India or a Muslim if you had grown up in Iraq." These wise men may well have come from somewhere around modern Iraq—a long way from the land of God's people. How does that help us to respond to the idea that people only follow the religion they grew up in? *(It is possible for people of other religions to start following Jesus. For anyone to start trusting and worshipping Jesus, it takes the Holy Spirit to do a miracle in them. Jesus is not just for the Jews. He's not just for people who live in "Christian countries". We can help anyone from any background to see Jesus.)*

Think and pray

Give thanks for the Christians you know from different countries and cultures. Pray that wise people would keep looking for Jesus.

Fun fact

"Wise men" or "magi" were the genius brainboxes of their day—the first to make new discoveries. Some were astrologers who studied whether the stars could explain events and history. Some tried to find meanings in dreams. Others studied ancient writings for prophecies and deep wisdom. And some tried to find the secret of magic and miracles. They wanted true wisdom.

⚠ OPTIONAL EXTRAS

Want to get adventurous?
Wait for a clear night and study the stars. Can you spot a constellation of stars?

Got time to chat?
We live in a time when so many of the people who celebrate Christmas don't worship the King whose birth they are remembering. Who could you pray for this Christmas to get to know Jesus? Can you think of ways of helping them to find out more about him?

Something more for the adults?
"Where is the one who has been born king of the Jews?" (Matthew 2 v 2, NIV)

"Above his head they placed the written charge against him: THIS IS JESUS, THE KING OF THE JEWS." (Matthew 27 v 37, NIV)

These verses show us for certain where the wise need to go to find the King of the Jews. Go to the cross and worship him now.

DAY 21

To Bethlehem

⊙ Where are we going today?
Herod, the religious leaders and the wise men discovered that God's promised King would be born in Bethlehem. Only the wise men went to find him.

Pray: Dear Father, please help us to be people who discover the truth about Jesus today and then live differently for him. Amen.

Ask a quick question
Is there a secret or amazing fact that only you know?

Link: Today we see the brightest religious minds find out the secret of where the promised King was to be born.

Today's story
- *Where are we in the Bible?* The mysterious men from the east have rolled into Jerusalem looking for the newborn king of the Jews. What is Herod going to say? Herod thinks he is the king of the Jews!

- *Look out for how they worked out where to find the Christ King.*

- *Read the passage. For young children, you could write the prophecy (v 6) on a piece of paper in an envelope, ready to open and read at the right moment, to show it's a message from God with the answer to their question.*

Matthew 2 v 4-8
⁴ Herod called a meeting of all the leading priests and teachers of the law. He asked them where the Christ would be born.

⁵ They answered, "In the town of Bethlehem in Judea. The prophet wrote about this in the Scriptures:

⁶ 'But you, Bethlehem, in the land of Judah,
    you are important among the rulers of Judah.

A ruler will come from you.
   He will be like a shepherd for my people, the Israelites.'" (Micah 5 v 2)

⁷ *Then Herod had a secret meeting with the wise men from the east. He learned from them the exact time they first saw the star.* ⁸ *Then Herod sent the wise men to Bethlehem. He said to them, "Go and look carefully to find the child. When you find him, come tell me. Then I can go worship him too."*

———————————— **?** ————————————

Question for 3s and 4s
Herod asked the priests and teachers about the new King. Where did they say the King would be born?

Question for 5-7s
How did they work that out? *(Verse 6 is a message that God gave the prophet Micah 800 years earlier, in plenty of time for the religious bigwigs to answer Herod's question!)*

Question for over-7s
Of all the people in this story who found out where the promised King could be found, which of them actually went to find him? Why do you think the others didn't go? *(Knowing the truth does not always lead to doing the right thing. There may have been hundreds in Herod's palace who heard that the promised King had been born in Bethlehem. Some of them knew their Bibles off by heart. But only the wise men believed, cared and went.)*

Question for teens
Did you catch the last line of the prophecy? "A ruler will come from you. He will be like a shepherd for my people." How would a ruler be different if they were like a shepherd? *(Most rulers want to stay in power as long as possible. Some make their nations richer, others make themselves richer. Imagine if a ruler wanted to <u>shepherd</u> their people; caring for the weakest, protecting the youngest and risking everything to keep them all safe.)*

———————————————————————————

Think and pray
Pray that your family will search for the truth and go looking for ways to serve Jesus. Give thanks that Jesus is our shepherd King.

! OPTIONAL EXTRAS

Want to get hiding?
Hide a play figure in another room and then go to find it! Can one of you play Herod, telling the others where to find it?

Got time to chat?
Why would someone find out the truth about Jesus but do nothing about it? In fact, we find out later that Herod secretly wanted to kill the newborn King

(Matthew 2 v 16). Why would Herod want to kill him? Today, why would some people find out who Jesus is but not want him in their lives?

Something more for the adults?

These verses are set in the palace of Herod, the king of the Jews, in the heart of Jerusalem, the ancient capital of God's people, with Herod surrounded by the most observant religious leaders. Just across the city, God's dwelling place, the Temple, was being rebuilt and refurbished. Amid all this scriptural knowledge, grand architecture and historic legacy, who rushed out of Jerusalem to find God's long-awaited promised King? Only these men from a pagan land went that day. It is right we remember them as the wise men. Will you be wise this Christmas and urgently seek Christ?

On your knees

⊙ Where are we going today?

When the wise men found Jesus there was joy, gifts and worship.

Pray: Dear Father, please help us to worship Jesus as the wise men did. Amen.

 ## Ask a quick question

Where would you most like to go? To another country? Into space? Under the sea? Or just down the road?

Link: Today we're joining the wise men as they finally arrive at the place they have travelled hundreds of miles to find.

Today's story

- *Where are we in the Bible?* The wise men had been travelling for months. When they finally arrived in Jerusalem, King Herod sent them six miles down the road to a tiny town called Bethlehem. Could God's final King really be *here?*

- *Look out for what the wise men did when they found the baby King.*

- *Read the passage. For young children: your child might be around the same age as Jesus in this story (he was probably a toddler). Can your child play the part of Jesus, as others discover him, bow down to him and present him with gifts?*

Matthew 2 v 9-12

⁹ *The wise men heard the king and then left. They saw the same star they had seen in the east. It went before them until it stopped above the place where the child was.* ¹⁰ *When the wise men saw the star, they were filled with joy.* ¹¹ *They went to the house where the child was and saw him with his mother, Mary. They bowed down and worshipped the child. They opened the gifts they brought for him. They gave him treasures of gold,*

frankincense, and myrrh. ¹² But God warned the wise men in a dream not to go back to Herod. So they went home to their own country by a different way.

———————————————— ❓ ————————————————

Question for 3s and 4s
What did the wise men do when they found Jesus?

Question for 5-7s
How did they find Jesus?

Question for over-7s
When you meet a normal toddler, you might pat them on the head or give them a hug or just wave and smile. Verse 11 says that when the wise men met Jesus, they "bowed down and worshipped the child." Why did these incredibly intelligent people greet this toddler like this?

Question for teens
We remember these men as the wise men. Which of their decisions that day were wise? *(The search, the gifts and the different route home—all wise. But bowing down to a toddler? That's only wise if this child will grow up to live such a life (and die such a death) that means he is God. Jesus did grow up to do those things—so the magi's decision to worship him was the wisest of all.)*

 Think and pray
Pray that we would understand what worshipping Jesus looks like for us today. Give thanks that the wise men were really wise, when almost no one else was.

❗ OPTIONAL EXTRAS

Want to get crafty?
Make a star from five straight branches, all the same length, and five elastic bands or pieces of string.

Got time to chat?

How do we decide what to do? Do we... do what everyone else does? Keep doing exactly the same thing? Avoid doing anything, and just step out of the action? It is hard to make wise choices like the wise men did. Talk about one of the choices you've made or will make today. Let's worship Jesus with our choices, and let's give Jesus everything that is precious to us, and see how our decisions become wiser.

Something more for the adults?

J.C. Ryle (1816-1900, Bishop of Liverpool) wrote, "These wise men believed in Christ when they had never seen him; but that was not all. They believed in him when the scribes and the Pharisees were unbelieving—but that again was not all. They believed in him when they saw him a little infant on Mary's knees, and worshipped him as King. This was the crowning point of their faith. They saw no miracles to convince them. They heard no teaching to persuade them. They beheld no signs of divinity and greatness to overawe them. They saw nothing but a new-born infant, helpless and weak, and needing a mother's care, like any of ourselves ... We read of no greater faith than this in the whole volume of the Bible ... Let us walk in the steps of their faith." (J.C. Ryle, *Expository thoughts on the Gospels: Matthew and Mark* (James Clarke & Co, 1983), p 12-13.)

DAY 23

A strong and gracious Saviour

⊙ Where are we going today?
Baby Jesus didn't stay a baby. Our Saviour grew up. What a man he became!

Pray: Dear Father, please help us to see that Jesus isn't just for Christmas. Thank you that Jesus grew up. Amen.

 Ask a quick question
What is your earliest memory? Do you remember being tiny?

Link: Today we see that baby Jesus grew up, like we all do. Let's see the young person he became.

Today's story

- *Where are we in the Bible?* Luke lets us see a little glimpse into Mary and Joseph's home as Jesus grew up in the years after the Christmas story.

- *Look out for* what Jesus was like as he got older.

- *Read the passage. For young children, use the picture on page 86 to show what these verses are telling us.*

Luke 2 v 39-40

³⁹ *Joseph and Mary finished doing everything that the law of the Lord commanded. Then they went home to Nazareth, their own town in Galilee.* ⁴⁰ *The little child began to grow up. He became stronger and wiser, and God's blessings were with him.*

?

Question for 3s and 4s
Who do you think the two people are in the picture?

Question for 5-7s
Do you think this picture is imagining Jesus when he was younger or older than you are now? What do these verses say Jesus was like at that age?

Question for over-7s
The angel told the shepherds that it was good news for all people that Jesus was born. Why is it good news that Jesus grew up, too? (*We needed him to grow up to show us what a great life looks like, to teach us about living for him, to die to save us, and then to rise again to defeat death. With Jesus, the good news keeps coming!*)

Question for teens
Why do you think most people prefer to only think and talk about Jesus as a baby? (*As a baby he is chubby, sweet, ordinary and safe. It's easier to ignore Jesus' power, his authority, his commands and his love for us when he doesn't speak. We don't need to obey a baby!*)

Think and pray
Thank God that Jesus knows exactly what it is like to be your age. Pray that you will become wiser as you get older.

! OPTIONAL EXTRAS

Want to get busy?
Find an old photo of yourself to see how much you have grown. Can you revisit the place where the photo was taken and recreate it today, to see how much you have grown up? How have you changed? Has your character changed?

Got time to chat?
Our children can sometimes feel alone and misunderstood. It's an extraordinary thought that Jesus was once actually our child's age. He knows what it is like to be 7 years, 4 months and 17 days old. He understands what it feels like to be wronged, to be teased, to feel alone, and to be misunderstood by his parents. In

a hard moment for your child, can you think together if Jesus felt like this? What might he have told himself?

Something more for the adults?

Read Luke 1 v 1-4 again. Give thanks that, like Theophilus, you are growing in your certainty of these things, as the Spirit works the truth into your heart. You know more of Christ than you once did, but oh—how much there is still to discover! Praise God that you will never be disappointed by him.

Back to
the manger

⊙ Where are we going today?

It is almost Christmas! Remember, it's all about the baby in the manger.

Pray: Dear Father, thank you for the excitement of Christmas. Please help us to celebrate the baby in the manger. Amen.

 ## Ask a quick question

Is there anything left to do before Christmas Day?

Link: With so much going on, let's take five minutes to think deeply about the reason for the season.

Today's story

- *Where are we in the Bible?* We're jumping back into the story we have already looked at, to finish getting ready for Christmas. This is the moment when the shepherds met Jesus Christ.

- *Look out for* why we are still celebrating Christmas 2,000 years later.

- *Read the passage.* For young children, can you wrap up a doll in a box to unwrap, in a moment of drama, as the shepherds find Jesus? The wrapping could be rough newspaper or a blanket.

Luke 2 v 16-18

[16] So the shepherds went quickly and found Mary and Joseph. [17] And the shepherds saw the baby lying in a feeding box. Then they told what the angels had said about this child. [18] Everyone was amazed when they heard what the shepherds said to them.

--- **?** ---

Question for 3s and 4s
What did the shepherds find?

Question for 5-7s
Why are we still celebrating this baby's birthday so many years later?

Question for over-7s
Take three deep breaths. Think carefully. If you could thank God for two things right now, what would they be?

Question for teens
Imagine you could send a text to the world right now. You have ten words and an emoji—max! What would you send?

 Think and pray
Tell God how you are feeling. Thank him.

! OPTIONAL EXTRAS

Want to get baking?
Get a packet of 24 biscuits (or bake some) and ice each one with the word or phrase from the Advent calendar on page 13. Look how far we have come! We have been on the adventure of Christmas.

Got time to chat?
Today will be full of preparation and excitement. Take a moment at bedtime to talk about how you will be celebrating Jesus' birthday tomorrow. Give thanks that Jesus' birth is the cause of all this joy.

Something more for the adults?
We have covered so much in these 24 sessions. Remember where we started? Luke said he was writing an orderly account "so that you may know the certainty of the things you have been taught." Can you think of something you feel more certain of about Jesus from reading Luke's excellent account?

DAY 25

Merry Christmas!

⊙ Where are we going today?
Merry Christmas! Let's celebrate the birth of Jesus.

Christmas Day is a blur for most families. And many of us love celebrating this great day with our church families. Perhaps there is a moment in the car on the way to church, during an afternoon walk or just before bed when you can thank God for his goodness to your family this Christmas. This session is to help you do that.

Ask a quick question

What is the moment you enjoyed the most on this Christmas adventure? Have you enjoyed learning something new?

Link: Let's thank God on this very special day for all that we have enjoyed and learned.

Think and pray

Pray short, quick prayers to thank God for what you have learned and enjoyed this Christmas.

Got time to chat?

When the presents have been opened, when the lunch has been eaten, when you collapse into bed—what will you thank God for? What will still be there tomorrow, when the bin is full of wrapping paper and empty boxes?

Something more for the adults?

Well done. You have held close to Christ. You have done your best to show Christ to your children this Advent. Join the shepherds in returning to normal life, "glorifying and praising God for all the things they had heard and seen, which were just as they had been told" (Luke 2 v 20, NIV).

Keep enjoying time with Jesus!

If you've enjoyed looking at God's word as a family this advent, why not keep going? *Meals With Jesus* invites you to nine mealtimes with the Lord, walking through Luke's Gospel to see more of who Jesus is and why he came.

faith in kids

exists to support churches and parents in raising children to trust in Jesus Christ eternally.

Point your kids in the right direction— when they're old they won't be lost.
Proverbs 22:6

Our simple, flexible resources enable churches and parents to confidently explore the Bible with children. Fun, relevant and truthful. Available from our website.

FOR CHURCHES:
Training, partnership and free ready-to-use downloadable resources for Sunday School, all age talks and holiday clubs

FOR FAMILIES:
Podcasts for parents, podcasts for families, books, videos and blog

faithinkids.org

faithinkids

thegoodbook
COMPANY

BIBLICAL | RELEVANT | ACCESSIBLE

At The Good Book Company, we are dedicated to helping Christians and local churches grow. We believe that God's growth process always starts with hearing clearly what he has said to us through his timeless word—the Bible.

Ever since we opened our doors in 1991, we have been striving to produce Bible-based resources that bring glory to God. We have grown to become an international provider of user-friendly resources to the Christian community, with believers of all backgrounds and denominations using our books, Bible studies, devotionals, evangelistic resources, and DVD-based courses.

We want to equip ordinary Christians to live for Christ day by day, and churches to grow in their knowledge of God, their love for one another, and the effectiveness of their outreach.

Call us for a discussion of your needs or visit one of our local websites for more information on the resources and services we provide.

Your friends at The Good Book Company

thegoodbook.com | thegoodbook.co.uk
thegoodbook.com.au | thegoodbook.co.nz
thegoodbook.co.in